Hello out there!

SPEAKING THROUGH PICTURES

Catherine Chambers
Illustrated by David Cockcroft

W
FRANKLIN WATTS
A Division of Grolier Publishing
NEW YORK • LONDON • HONG KONG • SYDNEY
DANBURY, CONNECTICUT

© Franklin Watts 1998
First American Edition 1998 by
Franklin Watts, A Division of Grolier Publishing
90 Sherman Turnpike, Danbury, CT 06816

Visit Franklin Watts on the Internet at:
http://publishing.grolier.com

Chambers, Catherine.
Speaking through Pictures / Catherine Chambers; illustrated by David Cockroft
    p.   cm. -- (Hello out there!)
Includes index.
Summary: Examines visual communications, from fine arts and photography
to signs and advertisements.
ISBN 0-531-14469-0 (lib. bdg.)   0-531-15347-9 (pbk.)
1. Visual communication--Juvenile literature.   [1. Visual communication.]
I. Cockroft, David, ill. II. Title. III. Series.
P93.5.C48   1998
302.23--dc21   97-44436
CIP
AC

Editor: Sarah Snashall
Series editor: Rachel Cooke
Designer: Melissa Alaverdy
Picture research: Sue Mennell

Printed in Belgium

Picture acknowledgements:
Cover photo: br AKG London/Musee du Louvre; bl Steve Shott
Advertising Archives p. 28
AKG London pp. 13b (Wera Ignatjewna Muchina),
17t (Erich Lessing/Galleria Nazionale delle Marche, Urbino), 18 (Private Collection),
19t (Musee Marmottan, Paris), 19b (Staalt. Kupferstichkabinett, Dresden)
(© The Andy Warhol Foundation for the Visual Arts, Inc./ARS, NY and DACS, London 1998), 20t, 26r
Bridgeman Art Library pp. 5 (National Gallery, London), 10 (Sculthorpe Church, Norfolk),
11 (Giraudon/Musee de la Tapisserie, Bayeux), 13t (Musee de l'Armee, Paris),
14 (Cathedral of Monreale, Sicily), 16 (Museu d'Art de Catalunya, Barcelona),
17b (British Library, London), 20b (Nasjonalgalleriet, Oslo)
(© The Munch Museum/The Munch-Ellingsen Group/DACS 1998),
21 (Marsden Archive), 29 (Victoria & Albert Museum, London)
Mary Evans Picture Library/? p.23
Ronald Grant Archive pp. 24, 26tl (© Walt Disney Co.)
Image Bank p. 7 (Leo Mason); Panos Pictures p. 15 (Neil Cooper)
Rex Features p. 13m; Steve Shott p. 9
Topham Picturepoint pp. 22 (Associated Press), 25 (NASA)

Contents

A World of Pictures

All around you are visual images — photographs and paintings, signs and **symbols**, patterns and carved shapes. You are surrounded with images in advertisements and magazines, on film, and on television. Pictures are an important part of communication in today's world.

What Do Visual Images Communicate?

Is it possible to communicate without words? Take a look at the visual images on this page. What do you think each one is trying to communicate? Is it a story or an idea? Is it a feeling or a piece of information? Does it look real or imaginary? Do you need the words to get the message?

Speaking Without Words

A piece of art can show something special. It can communicate an idea or feeling without using words. Pictures are also used in everyday life to show information quickly.

These pictures are a quick way of saying (from left to right): "environmentally friendly," "wash at 104°F" and "Beware: electricity."

Some images are simple, and they get across a very simple message, like these signs. ▼

The Skills of Communication

Artists, photographers, filmmakers, and **sculptors** have many tools to help them to communicate with their viewer. They can use color, light, **texture**, and even words to add meaning to the final image. They also make decisions about what to show and how to display it.

This picture tells a story. In it Saint George kills a dragon and saves the princess.

HELLO!

Most of the images you see in this book were created by men. Most women artists, sculptors, designers, and filmmakers have struggled to get their work shown. Do you think our visual world would be different if these women had been successful?

Think For Yourself

In this book you will discover how artists, photographers, sculptors, and designers try to communicate with you. But the most important thing is to decide for yourself how images make you feel. What do they mean to you?

Knowing at a Glance

Signs and symbols are some of the simplest forms of visual communication. They are designed to be eye-catching and instantly recognizable with bright colors and simple shapes.

Early Signs

Imagine that you need to communicate with someone but you can't speak his or her language. What do you do? For hundreds of years in America, the Plains Indians used a set of signs that they could all recognize — even though they didn't share the same language.

Signs and symbols were used as patterns on skins, cloth, and bark.

Signs for Safety

Road signs carry very important information. They need to be read easily even if you're traveling fast, and to be simple enough for anyone to understand what they mean.

They're made in simple shapes — round, rectangular, or triangular. The symbols inside them are simple, too. Bold, bright **primary colors** or black are used for the border or background.

PAINT POT!

Many warning signs are in yellow and black. This kind of color contrast can be found in nature to warn you away. Just think of bees and wasps!

Hidden Meaning

Some symbols are not instantly recognizable. You need to learn what these symbols **represent** in order to understand their full meaning. Carved and painted symbols are often used in religions to stand for something that you can't see, like love or hope.

In Islamic art, fruits show how God gives us all that we need.
▼

The star of David is a symbol for the Jewish faith.
▼

A white dove in Christian art is a symbol of peace.
▼

HELLO!

The dove has now become an international symbol of peace.

Selling with Symbols

Symbols can also stand for an organization, like the Red Cross. A symbol used in this way is called a logo. Logos are also used to sell products. They are displayed on packaging and advertising.

An athlete pushes off from her starting blocks. A famous logo is displayed on her bright sneakers.

Design Crazy!

Everything that is made is designed — from a pencil to a computer, from a fork to a forklift truck. Things just don't work properly if they haven't been designed well. They don't look attractive, either.

Design Tools

But now take a look at the visual images around you. You will see that pictures, newspapers, magazines, books, posters, cards, postcards, logos, and packaging all have been designed. The designer chooses the colors and layout. Any words also have to be designed — the designer has to choose the right sizes and styles of letters.

Which of these invitations would attract you to the fancy dress party?

Bookman
Helvetica Thin
Stone Sans Serif
Times
Lebensjoy Bold
Palatino
Zaph Chancery
Gill Sans Serif
Mead Bold

▲

Which of these typefaces, or fonts, would you choose for a comic?

HELLO!
Some designs haven't changed for over a hundred years! Coca Cola is one — the loopy lettering is still the same. The Ford Motor Company's logo hasn't changed, either. Keeping things the same makes the product seem reliable — you can trust it.

Designed to Attract You

Take a look at different types of packaging. What do you think when you look at them? Do you judge a product by its box or bag? Packaging is designed to attract different groups of people.

Presents are for special people. You can choose the best wrapping paper for each one. Which ones attract you? Do you know people who might prefer the others?

Simple packaging with a cool color makes products seem safe and reliable.

The Design Revolution

The computer has revolutionized design. Images can be altered many times until they are almost perfect.

PAINT POT!
Color is an important part of packaging design. Blue is often used for medicines and soap powders. It makes the product look clean and reliable.

At the switch of a button, designers can change the color and shape of an image. They can alter the typeface of lettering. Computers allow designers to work really fast.

Telling a Story

Many people today can read other people's stories and ideas. Before writing and reading became widespread, pictures were often used to record stories or events.

The First Stories

In Africa, Australia, and Europe, early humans left pictures painted on rock. Some told stories of hunting or battles. Others showed ancient religious beliefs.

TOOL-BOX!

The ancient Greeks used their myths to decorate vases. This vase shows Theseus killing the terrible beast named the Minotaur.

Religious Stories

Hundreds of years ago most people couldn't read the stories from their religious books. Scenes from these important stories were used to decorate the walls and windows of religious buildings. This helped people to remember the stories they had heard.

This stained-glass window from a church tells the story of Ruth, who gathered wheat by the side of a field.

This part of the Bayeux tapestry shows King Harold eating before leaving England for France. You can see how people dressed, and how they undressed to wade out to the boat! What did they take with them?

Looking at History

When you see an old painting, take a look at the background. It will give you an idea of when and where the story in the picture took place. It's a bit like the scenery in a play. Then look at the small details — the furniture or the things people are holding. These are like the **props** in a play.

Get Drawing!

Draw a picture of a friend. Put things in the background that show what hobbies your friend has or which bands he or she likes.

Words and Pictures

Pictures can illustrate a written story or instruction. They add atmosphere to a story or give an impression of what a character looks like. Illustrations help us to understand instructions, too. How do the illustrations in this book add to your understanding of the words?

WASHER / DRYER
Model DZ-3500

M A N U A L

Images of Power

Many of the images we see have been paid for by rich and powerful people. The cost of an object, its size, visible riches, and beauty can **glorify** the person who paid for it. The object can show a person's power and wealth.

The Power of Sculpture

Stone sphinxes are carved out of solid rock. Most show the power of ancient Egyptian rulers about 5,000 years ago. The heads look like different kings and queens — or sometimes they look like a ram or a hawk. The body is always a lion. Sphinxes are also found in other cultures, from Roman to Central American Mayan.

This sphinx protects a pyramid tomb. Some sphinxes were placed beside huge gateways or temples.

TOOL-BOX!

Some of the sculptures in Egypt were covered in gold. This really showed the poor people of Egypt who was important.

Money Makes Art

There has been a long tradition of rich people paying artists to paint for them. These people expected their wealth and power to show in the portraits. Expensive clothes and fine buildings were often painted. Poor people were placed beneath the rich. In a way, art was a fashion statement of the times — paintings were designed to show off!

This portrait of Napoleon shows his wealth and power. He has just been crowned emperor. The painter has used lots of red and gold.

Today, glamorous pictures in glossy magazines seem to show off, too.

HELLO!
Some of the greatest collections of art have been made by rich and famous people. Many have given works of art to public art galleries and museums.

Big and Bold

In the 1930s and 1940s, the Russian dictator Joseph Stalin ordered huge **murals**, statues, and posters to be placed in public places. They showed smiling, healthy, hard-working people. This visual propaganda made it seem as if everyone was happy under Stalin's rule, but many people suffered. Propaganda often tries to persuade people that everything's all right — when it isn't.

This statue uses strong, chunky shapes and materials. It was made during Stalin's rule.

Images of Faith

As we have seen, people used art to tell religious stories. For thousands of years people have also expressed their **devotion** to God and to gods and goddesses through paintings, sculptures, tapestries, buildings, and **stained-glass windows**.

The goodness and importance of Hindu gods and goddesses are represented by statues. Here, a Hindu makes an offering (Puja).

Filling with Awe

Throughout history people have decorated their places of worship using the most expensive and impressive materials they can. This shows both their own devotion and the power of their god. The beauty of the religious buildings and the rich colors used to decorate them are designed to fill people with awe.

This mosaic was made over 800 years ago in Sicily. Mosaics are pictures or patterns made out of tiny pieces of colored stone. Here, Jesus Christ is shown as the ruler of the Universe. There are also saints and the Virgin Mary. Jesus Christ is at the top and towers over the saints and also over any worshipers in the church.

HELLO!
Visual images are an important part of religious ceremony. In parts of Africa, carved masks have been worn to mark the stages of a person's life or death.

Strong Beliefs

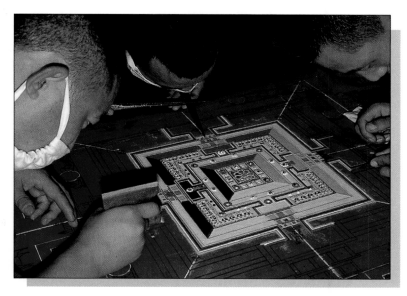

Many people use art to express their beliefs. Here you can see Buddhist monks patiently making a picture out of colored sand. These pictures are called mandalas.

The design and symbols represent the heavens or sacred places. The picture won't last, but the monks have shown discipline and devotion in making it.

Get Drawing!

Make a stained-glass window!

1. Cut the shape of a long or round window from a piece of black paper.

2. Now cut out from your window small shapes or symbols that mean something important to you. Leave gaps between the shapes.

3. Stick different colored tissue paper behind the gaps.

4. Hang your colored window in front of natural light.

Real Shapes

Since the first time a person picked up a paintbrush, artists have tried to find ways of showing the world around them. Some artists have tried to make their paintings look as realistic as possible.

Light and Shade

Sculptures and carvings are formed into real shapes that you can feel and hold. But in flat photographs and paintings, you need to use light and shade to give an idea of shape. Light and shade show an object's different surfaces.

In this painting you can see how the light hits Saint Francis of Assisi at an angle. Some parts of his gown are in pale shades, where the light hits them. Others are darker, where the folds of the gown are in shadow. This makes the painting look **three-dimensional**.

TOOL-BOX!

The artists who painted the Chauvet caves thousands of years ago used curves and lumps in the rocks to make their works look three-dimensional. This is like a combination of painting and sculpture.

A Problem of Size

Pictures look even more real if they have the correct **perspective**. This means that objects appear at the right distance from each other. The picture as a whole has shape and **depth**.

In this painting the **horizon** really looks a long way away. To achieve this, close buildings are drawn larger. As objects get farther away, they are drawn gradually smaller.

HELLO!
The laws of perspective were perfected by an Italian architect named Brunelleschi (1377–1446). He used the mathematical skills of mapmakers and astronomers.

Flat Art

Sometimes, artists show quite flat images on purpose. Chinese and Japanese **landscape** painting reveals the beauty of the countryside through simple, clear shapes. There is only a little shading. The flatness actually gives certain images strength and **impact**.

The shapes are simple. The scene looks quite flat. Yet this Japanese painting looks peaceful and beautiful.

True Colors

Light and shade can give shape as we have seen. But the choice and **depth** of color can also make visual images look true to life. Color can also be used to make things really stand out.

Making It Real

Layers of **oil paint**, **acrylic paint**, and **gouache** give thick textures. They are also opaque — you can't see through them. This gives deep, rich colors.

In this oil painting the thick, deep colors help to make the objects look quite solid. The colors and light are realistic, helping to make the scene true to life. Smooth brushstrokes make it look almost like a photograph.

Delicate Colors

HELLO!
In Japanese and Chinese landscape paintings, you can often see a white path leading from Earth up to the heavens. It represents life leading toward death and peace.

In some paintings, the colors look real but a bit pale. This kind of painting often uses **watercolor** or **tempera** paints. They're translucent — you can see through them. They give a soft, delicate quality. If you mix oil paints with lots of **turpentine**, it thins the paint. This also makes a painting soft and delicate. You can compare the fine, pale Japanese painting on page 17 with the richer painting on this page.

Making a Splash!

In the first picture, we saw how objects and the light on them look believable. We have also seen how light and shade give things more shape (see page 16). But color also draws attention to objects or people.

In this blue scene the sun and the boats are pointed out by **dramatic** black and red. The painting is by Claude Monet.

Breaking the Rules

Many artists have painted things in unusual colors. The pop artists who painted in the 1950s and 1960s liked to paint art that was different from what people thought art should be. They painted objects from modern life and often used bright colors.

This is Andy Warhol's painting of the famous movie star Marilyn Monroe. What do the colors do to the image?

PAINT POT!

Over 100 years ago artists were very excited about new uses of color. They felt free to paint things the color they wanted to. The artist Henri Matisse said, "When I paint green, it doesn't mean grass; when I paint blue, it doesn't mean sky."

Moods

Sometimes, artists and photographers want to capture the feeling of the scene as well as what it looks like. They want to give an **impression** of what a scene feels like to the viewer.

Real Feelings

Some artists paint expressions on faces to show how the characters feel. Positions of the body and especially the hands can also show feeling and mood.

You can see anger and violence in the face and body of this actor. This is a Japanese painting, over 150 years old.

Expressing a Feeling

About 100 years ago, European and American artists wanted to paint what they felt instead of what they saw. They were called expressionists because they expressed moods. The mood of an expressionist painter, or of a time or place, is shown by using different textures and shades of paint.

This picture is called *The Scream*. Nothing in it looks real, but you can sense fear and trouble.

Moody Films

The mood of a photograph or film can be changed by lighting or the way the film is **exposed** or developed. The picture can be made light or dark. The contrast between black and white can be harsh or soft. The texture of the picture can look smooth or grainy. It can be slightly blurred to make the picture look dreamy and romantic.

This picture of Whitby Abbey in Yorkshire looks spooky. The building seems overpowering. The clouds look threatening.

Color filters can alter shades quite dramatically. An orange filter can make the sky look stormy.

Out of This World

A mood of rebellion was created by pop art (see page 19). Pop art was influenced by advertising. It aimed to shock — or make people laugh! Artists painted everyday objects such as boxes of detergent. They used splashes or blotches of color. Images of movie and pop idols, and solid objects were stuck on the canvas.

Get Drawing!

Be a pop artist! Make a collage.

Cut out advertisements, modern objects, and pictures of pop stars from magazines and catalogs. Glue them on a large sheet of paper and add your own drawings or writing to the final image.

POP ART!

Instant Pictures!

As we have seen, photographs can be a powerful art form. But photographs are more widely used to give a clear, instant image of a time, a place, people, or events. They are the most common way of recording the world around us.

HELLO!

Black-and-white photography was invented about 150 years ago. The first commercial color process was made in 1907. But it wasn't until 1935 that the first popular color film was made.

We use photographs to help our memory. We record holidays and family events, such as weddings.

The Good . . .

People have to sit for hours to have their portrait painted. But the photographer can take just a few seconds. This means that people can appear more natural. Sometimes you don't even know the camera is there!

. . . the Bad and the Ugly

For over 100 years photography has given us pictures of war and disasters. This is called photojournalism. These shock us with images of the terrible things that go on around the world.

This photo of a child hurt in a bombed building shocks us because the victim is so young and helpless. It is a picture that many people remember because it appeared in newspapers and on television all over the world. But why do we see this kind of picture? Is it to inform us? Is it to raise sympathy — or even money? Is it to make us buy newspapers?

Twisting the Truth?

All photographs are planned. The photographer composes the picture within a frame. Imagine a scene of rolling green hills with a stone quarry to one side.

▲ If the photographer wants a picture of natural beauty, the quarry will be left out.

◀ If a picture of industry is needed, the rolling hills will just have to go.

The Camera Never Lies!

Most of us have seen photographs of UFOs — unidentified flying objects. Or have we seen them? Some images use trick photography. A false object is developed on top of a real-life scene. Trick photography is often used in advertising.

This is an old photograph called *The Cottingley Fairies*. It is a fake, but people really believed in it at the time.

The World on a Screen

Over 100 years ago, people were astonished to see stories, ideas, feelings, and events rolling before their eyes! Film and video have meant that the same visual images now appear all over the world.

Silent Stories

Early moving pictures had no sound. Scenery and props gave an idea of when and where the action was taking place. The actors showed all action and feeling by moving their bodies and faces in an **exaggerated** way.

Scene 3 Take 2 "RAGS To RICHES"

Sound and Vision

Now, words and music are added to the effect of a film. This means that acting can be more natural. Music is chosen especially for each film — soft music for romantic scenes, dramatic music for death or adventure. Rolls of thunder, roaring traffic, or the soft sound of a running stream all add to the **atmosphere** of a film.

Scary music and dinosaur roars add to the fear in the film *The Lost World: Jurassic Park*.

The World in Our Homes

Fear, fun, sport, science, worship, war — all these things can now be seen at the press of a button in our homes. With satellite pictures we now see events as they are happening all over the world. Video and satellite TV mean that we have even more choice about what we see, too. Now, there is interactive television — the audience can actually take part in programs.

TOOL-BOX!

How do sound and vision run exactly together? At first a **magnetic sound track** ran along the side of the filmstrip. Nowadays, an **optical sound track** is used.

News pictures bring us historical ▶ events. Here Edwin Aldrin walks on the surface of the moon.

BUY NOW!

$49·99

$62·99

PHONE

▲

In some countries, you can even do your shopping by choosing products shown on television.

Cartoon Creations

Cartoons can show ideas and feelings without words. Often they use exaggerated features. They have given us characters, like Mickey Mouse. They can make us laugh. But they have often shown a cruel side, too.

Making Fun

Political cartoons make fun of important people. Their faces and bodies are drawn with all the defects — the things we like to hide. Everything is exaggerated. People can see exactly what the cartoonist means, without needing to read words.

Over 100 years ago, this cartoon made fun of Charles Darwin. He tried to persuade people that humans come from a type of ape.

Too Cruel to Be True

The violence in many cartoons is exaggerated. The characters never look really hurt. We do not seem to connect this with real pain.

Animation

In the 1930s moving cartoons really brought the characters to life. Like silent movies, the characters' exaggerated movements tell the story without speech (see page 24). Many artists work as a team on cartoon films. They draw the action on clear celluloid. Each frame shows a tiny increase in movement. When all the movements are run together, the action is fast and smooth.

HELLO!

With the use of computer technology, cartoon characters now appear successfully alongside real actors in films. In 1988 the film *Who Framed Roger Rabbit?* paved the way. But the cartoon effects became even more realistic in *Space Jam*, made in 1996.

Get Drawing!

Make a flip book with a moving cartoon in it.

1. Use a small pad of paper.

2. Take a simple shape and movement, like a bouncing ball. Draw the ball on the ground on the first page, or frame. Then draw it bouncing up very slightly in each of the next few frames. Draw the ball coming down again.

3. Then flick the pages of the book and watch the ball bounce!

Sell, Sell, Sell!

Advertisements really grab your attention. They are big and bold. Some are enormous. But whatever the size, they are designed to persuade you to spend your money!

Life Is Good

Images of beautiful scenery and smiling faces are the cheerful side of photography. These pictures communicate that life is good. We look back at happy holidays, when the sun always shines.

Travel agents use this type of picture in brochures to lure us to faraway places.

Making You Feel Good

Some advertisements try to make you believe that you could be like the images they show. You, too, could be smart or cool if you buy the product! Other advertisements try to scare you into buying something, such as a toothpaste. Advertisements for sweet foods try to make them look too tempting to resist. They use mouth-watering pictures, like this one.

HELLO! The printing press was invented in 1450. Since then, written **slogans** have become an important part of advertising. Mass printing has meant that the same message can be seen in many places.

The Art of Persuasion

Some advertisements show funny situations to grab your attention. Others attract you with fashionable colors and stylish shapes. Still others use just a few words on a large space of a single color, often black or red.

This is a 1924 advertisement for the London underground railway. Clear, bright colors and strong lines make visiting London by subway seem very attractive.

BRIGHTEST LONDON
IS BEST REACHED BY
UNDERGROUND

HELLO!
One of the first known advertisements was painted on a wall in Rome over 2,000 years ago. It offered houses for rent. Nowadays these types of advertisement are huge posters stuck onto billboards.

There's No Escape!

Advertisements appear everywhere! Take a look in newspapers and magazines, on television, delivery trucks, shopping bags, packaging, stickers, and wrapping paper.

Even the sky isn't safe! There are advertisements on balloons and banners trailed by airplanes. There's even skywriting advertisements written in clouds of gas.

Glossary

acrylic paint: a thick paint made out of chemical pigments. You can thin it with water or use it in thick blobs or layers.

atmosphere: the mood that an image creates. It could be peaceful, frightening, happy, and so on.

depth: depth in color means that the colour is rich; depth in perspective means that a picture looks three-dimensional.

devotion: giving something a lot of your time, care, and attention.

dramatic: an image that gets your attention quickly. Maybe it has unusual colors. Perhaps it is very large.

exaggerated: a normal image that is made to appear unusual. It could be made a lot larger, smaller, rounder, thinner, brighter, and so on.

exposed: in photography, this means letting a certain amount of light through the lens of your camera onto the film. You need light to imprint an image on the film. Or it can mean letting light onto the film negative to make a print.

glorify: to give special praise to someone or something.

gouache: a thick paint traditionally made with pigments, honey, and gum.

horizon: far into the distance — where the sun seems to rise and set.

impact: how much an image grabs your attention. A strong impact means you have reacted quickly and with great feeling to an image.

impressions: images that are not exactly true to life. They concentrate on showing feelings and moods.

landscape: an image that shows scenery rather than close objects.

magnetic sound track: a metal strip set along the side of a moving film. It carries sound signals.

murals: paintings on walls.

oil paint: a thick paint made with natural or man-made pigments and oils. It can be thinned with turpentine.

optical sound track: a sound strip set along the side of a moving film. It carries visual sound signals.

perspective: the use of space, size, light, and shade to make an image true to life. Shape and distance look real.

pigments: colors used to make paints and crayons. They are usually powders that are then mixed with oils or gums.

primary colors: the colors that can be used to make other colors. With pigments, these colors are red, yellow, and blue. Primary colors of light are red, green, and blue.

props: objects used by actors in a play or film to make the situation feel more life-like. Furniture, tools, and other pieces of equipment are examples.

represent: to stand for something else.

sculptors: artists that shape materials into solid objects.

slogans: words that are frequently used to describe a product or an idea.

stained-glass windows: windows with colored glass panes. The panes usually make a pattern or a picture.

symbols: shapes or letters that have a special meaning. They can represent an idea or a group of people.

tapestry: a picture or pattern made out of woven colored thread.

tempera paint: a type of paint made from mixing pigment with egg.

texture: the feel of something. It could be rough, smooth, soft, hard, and so on.

three-dimensional: describes something that isn't flat but has height, width and depth. A flat image that has been drawn to look as if it has shape can also be said to be three-dimensional.

turpentine: an oil that comes from conifer trees. It is used to thin oil paints. It also helps them to dry.

watercolor paint: a thin paint made from pigment and gum. It can be thinned even more by adding water.

Paintings used in this book:
cover *Mona Lisa*
by Leonardo da Vinci (1451–1519)
p.5 *St. George and the Dragon*
by Paolo Uccello (1397–1475)
p.13 top *The Coronation of Napoleon I*
by Jean-Auguste Ingres (1780–1867)
p.13 bottom *Statue of a worker and a collective farmer*
by Wera Ignatjewna (1889–1953)
p.16 *Saint Francis of Assisi*
by Francisco de Zurbaran (1598–1664)
p.17 top *The Ideal Town*
by Piero della Francesca (1410/20–1492)
p.17 bottom *Hisaka in the Sayo mountains*
by Ando or Utagawa Hiroshige (1797–1858)
p.18 *Still life with fruits and goblet*
by Hermann Koch (born 1856)
p.19 top *Impression, soleil levant*
(Impression, sun rising)
by Claude Monet (1840–1926)
p.19 bottom *Marilyn Monroe*
by Andy Warhol (1928–1987)
p.20 *Kabuki actor*
by Kunisada Utagawa (1786–1865)
p.20 bottom *The Scream*
by Edvard Munch (1863-1944)
p.29 *Brightest London is Best Reached by Underground*
1924 by the Dangerfield Co.

Index